AF875578

Marty Zweig's Investing Rules

1. The trend is your friend: Don't fight the tape.
2. Let profits run, take losses quickly.
3. If you buy for a reason and that reason is discounted or is no longer valid, sell!
4. If the values don't make sense, ten don't participate (2+2=4)
5. The cheap get cheaper, the dear get dearer.
6. Don't fight the Fed.
7. Every indicator eventually bites the dust.
8. Adapt to change
9. Don't let your opinion on what should happen bias your trading strategy.
10. Don't blame your mistakes on the market.
11. Don't play all the time.
12. The market is not efficient, but it is still tough to beat.
13. You'll never know all the answers.
14. If you can't sleep at night, reduce your positions or get out.
15. Don't put too much faith in the "experts".
16. Don't focus too much on short-term information flows.
17. Beware "new era" thinking (i.e. "it's different this time because...")

Source: 2022 Stock Trader's Almanac

MY INDICATORS

Primary Indicator: ______________ Secondary Indicator: ______________

Tertiary Indicator: ______________ Quaternary Indicator: ______________

BASED ON MY RESEARCH:

The most activity occurs:

Time: ______________________________

Day(s): ______________________________

The best timeframe is ______________________________

The 2nd best timeframe is ______________________________

The 3rd best timeframe is ______________________________

The best period is ______________________________

The 2nd best period is ______________________________

The 3rd best period is ______________________________

I will Short when ______________________________

____

I will Long when ______________________________

____

I will not do anything when ______________________________

____

____

____

MY PLAN

Instrument: ________

Yearly Monetary Goal: $________________ = ___________ Points / Ticks

Monthly Goal: $________________ = ___________ Points / Ticks

Weekly Goal: $________________ = ___________ Points / Ticks

Beginning Balance: $ ____________________________________

Big Target (your swing trade)

Risk: ____________ Reward: __________ Stoploss: _______

I will use _______________ timeframe.

I will only go for this target when: ______________________________

____

____

____

Medium Target (your intraday/swing trade)

Risk: ____________ Reward: __________ Stoploss: _______

I will use _______________ timeframe.

I will only go for this target when: ______________________________

____

____

____

Small Target (your scalping trade)

Risk: ____________ Reward: __________ Stoploss: _______

I will use _______________ timeframe.

I will only go for this target when: ______________________________

____

____

____

Trade Tracker

Month: ____________

☐ Big Target ☐ Medium Target ☐ Small Target	☐ Big Target ☐ Medium Target ☐ Small Target	☐ Big Target ☐ Medium Target ☐ Small Target	☐ Big Target ☐ Medium Target ☐ Small Target	☐ Big Target ☐ Medium Target ☐ Small Target
☐ Big Target ☐ Medium Target ☐ Small Target	☐ Big Target ☐ Medium Target ☐ Small Target	☐ Big Target ☐ Medium Target ☐ Small Target	☐ Big Target ☐ Medium Target ☐ Small Target	☐ Big Target ☐ Medium Target ☐ Small Target
☐ Big Target ☐ Medium Target ☐ Small Target	☐ Big Target ☐ Medium Target ☐ Small Target	☐ Big Target ☐ Medium Target ☐ Small Target	☐ Big Target ☐ Medium Target ☐ Small Target	☐ Big Target ☐ Medium Target ☐ Small Target
☐ Big Target ☐ Medium Target ☐ Small Target	☐ Big Target ☐ Medium Target ☐ Small Target	☐ Big Target ☐ Medium Target ☐ Small Target	☐ Big Target ☐ Medium Target ☐ Small Target	☐ Big Target ☐ Medium Target ☐ Small Target
☐ Big Target ☐ Medium Target ☐ Small Target	☐ Big Target ☐ Medium Target ☐ Small Target	☐ Big Target ☐ Medium Target ☐ Small Target	☐ Big Target ☐ Medium Target ☐ Small Target	☐ Big Target ☐ Medium Target ☐ Small Target

Trade Tracker

Month: ______________

☐ Big Target ☐ Medium Target ☐ Small Target	☐ Big Target ☐ Medium Target ☐ Small Target	☐ Big Target ☐ Medium Target ☐ Small Target	☐ Big Target ☐ Medium Target ☐ Small Target	☐ Big Target ☐ Medium Target ☐ Small Target
☐ Big Target ☐ Medium Target ☐ Small Target	☐ Big Target ☐ Medium Target ☐ Small Target	☐ Big Target ☐ Medium Target ☐ Small Target	☐ Big Target ☐ Medium Target ☐ Small Target	☐ Big Target ☐ Medium Target ☐ Small Target
☐ Big Target ☐ Medium Target ☐ Small Target	☐ Big Target ☐ Medium Target ☐ Small Target	☐ Big Target ☐ Medium Target ☐ Small Target	☐ Big Target ☐ Medium Target ☐ Small Target	☐ Big Target ☐ Medium Target ☐ Small Target
☐ Big Target ☐ Medium Target ☐ Small Target	☐ Big Target ☐ Medium Target ☐ Small Target	☐ Big Target ☐ Medium Target ☐ Small Target	☐ Big Target ☐ Medium Target ☐ Small Target	☐ Big Target ☐ Medium Target ☐ Small Target
☐ Big Target ☐ Medium Target ☐ Small Target	☐ Big Target ☐ Medium Target ☐ Small Target	☐ Big Target ☐ Medium Target ☐ Small Target	☐ Big Target ☐ Medium Target ☐ Small Target	☐ Big Target ☐ Medium Target ☐ Small Target

7 Deadly Sins of Trading

1. Sloth: The belief that trading is easy money
2. Lust: Spending profits instead of compounding capital
3. Pride: Inability to admit you're wrong
4. Wrath: Revenge trading
5. Greed: Trying to get rich quick
6. Envy: Worrying about others
7. Gluttony: Trading too big

Source: Steven Burn's Twitter (@SJosephBurns)

Date: ________ Day: ________ Time: ______ Instrument: _____

Pre-Trade Checklist

☐ Reviewed News

☐ Reviewed VIX: ______

☐ Reviewed Fear/Greed Index: ___________

☐ My Target: ________

☐ Reviewed Volume: ___________

☐ Reviewed Open Interest: ___________

☐ Reviewed Direction: ___________

☐ My Risk/Reward: ________

☐ Am I trading during Prime Hours or a clear trend?: ________

Trade

Big Timeframe: ___________

↑ ↔ ↓

Medium Timeframe: __________

↑ ↔ ↓

Small Timeframe: ___________

↑ ↔ ↓

	Contracts	Position	Entry Time	Entry Price	Exit Price	W/L
1.	________	_______	_________	_________	________	___
2.	________	_______	_________	_________	________	___
3.	________	_______	_________	_________	________	___
4.	________	_______	_________	_________	________	___
5.	________	_______	_________	_________	________	___

Results

Today's Profit Factor: ______

Today's PnL: ________________

Cumulative Profit Factor: ______

Cumulative PnL: ________________

Post-Trade

Did I follow my plan? What went right/wrong?

What were my emotions & mental during the trade?

What lessons did I learn?

What questions do I have after today's trades?

Was I correct in trading today or should I have just watched today?

Date: ________ Day: ________ Time: ______ Instrument: _____

Pre-Trade Checklist

☐ Reviewed News

☐ Reviewed Volume: ____________

☐ Reviewed VIX: ______

☐ Reviewed Open Interest: ____________

☐ Reviewed Fear/Greed Index: ___________

☐ Reviewed Direction: ____________

☐ My Target: ________

☐ My Risk/Reward: ________

☐ Am I trading during Prime Hours or a clear trend?: ________

Trade

Big Timeframe:	Medium Timeframe:	Small Timeframe:
___________	___________	___________
↑ ↔ ↓	↑ ↔ ↓	↑ ↔ ↓

	Contracts	Position	Entry Time	Entry Price	Exit Price	W/L
1.	________	________	________	________	________	____
2.	________	________	________	________	________	____
3.	________	________	________	________	________	____
4.	________	________	________	________	________	____
5.	________	________	________	________	________	____

Results

Today's Profit Factor: ______ Today's PnL: ________________

Cumulative Profit Factor: ______ Cumulative PnL: ________________

Post-Trade

Did I follow my plan? What went right/wrong?

What were my emotions & mental during the trade?

What lessons did I learn?

What questions do I have after today's trades?

Was I correct in trading today or should I have just watched today?

Date: ________ Day: ________ Time: ______ Instrument: _____

Pre-Trade Checklist

☐ Reviewed News

☐ Reviewed Volume: ____________

☐ Reviewed VIX: ______

☐ Reviewed Open Interest: ____________

☐ Reviewed Fear/Greed Index: ___________

☐ Reviewed Direction: ____________

☐ My Target: ________

☐ My Risk/Reward: ________

☐ Am I trading during Prime Hours or a clear trend?: _______

Trade

Big Timeframe:	Medium Timeframe:	Small Timeframe:
___________	___________	___________
↑ ↔ ↓	↑ ↔ ↓	↑ ↔ ↓

1.	Contracts	Position	Entry Time	Entry Price	Exit Price	W/L
	________	_______	_________	_________	________	___
2.	Contracts	Position	Entry Time	Entry Price	Exit Price	W/L
	________	_______	_________	_________	________	___
3.	Contracts	Position	Entry Time	Entry Price	Exit Price	W/L
	________	_______	_________	_________	________	___
4.	Contracts	Position	Entry Time	Entry Price	Exit Price	W/L
	________	_______	_________	_________	________	___
5.	Contracts	Position	Entry Time	Entry Price	Exit Price	W/L
	________	_______	_________	_________	________	___

Results

Today's Profit Factor: ______ Today's PnL: _________________

Cumulative Profit Factor: ______ Cumulative PnL: _________________

Post-Trade

Did I follow my plan? What went right/wrong?

What were my emotions & mental during the trade?

What lessons did I learn?

What questions do I have after today's trades?

Was I correct in trading today or should I have just watched today?

Date: ________ Day: ________ Time: ______ Instrument: _____

Pre-Trade Checklist

☐ Reviewed News

☐ Reviewed Volume: ___________

☐ Reviewed VIX: ______

☐ Reviewed Open Interest: ___________

☐ Reviewed Fear/Greed Index: __________

☐ Reviewed Direction: ___________

☐ My Target: _______

☐ My Risk/Reward: _______

☐ Am I trading during Prime Hours or a clear trend?: _______

Trade

Big Timeframe: __________ ↑ ↔ ↓

Medium Timeframe: _________ ↑ ↔ ↓

Small Timeframe: __________ ↑ ↔ ↓

	Contracts	Position	Entry Time	Entry Price	Exit Price	W/L
1.						
2.						
3.						
4.						
5.						

Results

Today's Profit Factor: ______ Today's PnL: _________________

Cumulative Profit Factor: ______ Cumulative PnL: ________________

Post-Trade

Did I follow my plan? What went right/wrong?

....

....

....

....

What were my emotions & mental during the trade?

....

....

....

....

....

....

....

What lessons did I learn?

....

....

....

....

....

What questions do I have after today's trades?

....

....

....

....

....

Was I correct in trading today or should I have just watched today?

....

....

....

....

....

Date: ________ Day: ________ Time: ______ Instrument: _____

Pre-Trade Checklist

☐ Reviewed News

☐ Reviewed Volume: ____________

☐ Reviewed VIX: ______

☐ Reviewed Open Interest: ____________

☐ Reviewed Fear/Greed Index: __________

☐ Reviewed Direction: ____________

☐ My Target: ________

☐ My Risk/Reward: ________

☐ Am I trading during Prime Hours or a clear trend?: _______

Trade

Big Timeframe: __________ ↑ ↔ ↓

Medium Timeframe: __________ ↑ ↔ ↓

Small Timeframe: __________ ↑ ↔ ↓

1.	Contracts ______	Position ______	Entry Time ______	Entry Price ______	Exit Price ______	W/L ___
2.	Contracts ______	Position ______	Entry Time ______	Entry Price ______	Exit Price ______	W/L ___
3.	Contracts ______	Position ______	Entry Time ______	Entry Price ______	Exit Price ______	W/L ___
4.	Contracts ______	Position ______	Entry Time ______	Entry Price ______	Exit Price ______	W/L ___
5.	Contracts ______	Position ______	Entry Time ______	Entry Price ______	Exit Price ______	W/L ___

Results

Today's Profit Factor: ______ Today's PnL: ________________

Cumulative Profit Factor: ______ Cumulative PnL: ________________

Post-Trade

Did I follow my plan? What went right/wrong?

What were my emotions & mental during the trade?

What lessons did I learn?

What questions do I have after today's trades?

Was I correct in trading today or should I have just watched today?

Homework:
Types of Trading

- ☐ News trading strategy
- ☐ End-of-day trading strategy
- ☐ Swing trading strategy
- ☐ Day trading strategy
- ☐ Trend trading strategy
- ☐ Scalping trading strategy
- ☐ Position trading strategy

Source: https://www.cmcmarkets.com/en/trading-guides/trading-strategies

Date: ________ Day: ________ Time: ______ Instrument: ______

Pre-Trade Checklist

☐ Reviewed News

☐ Reviewed Volume: __________

☐ Reviewed VIX: ______

☐ Reviewed Open Interest: __________

☐ Reviewed Fear/Greed Index: __________

☐ Reviewed Direction: __________

☐ My Target: ________

☐ My Risk/Reward: ________

☐ Am I trading during Prime Hours or a clear trend?: ________

Trade

Big Timeframe:	Medium Timeframe:	Small Timeframe:
__________	__________	__________
↑ ↔ ↓	↑ ↔ ↓	↑ ↔ ↓

	Contracts	Position	Entry Time	Entry Price	Exit Price	W/L
1.	________	________	________	________	________	____
2.	________	________	________	________	________	____
3.	________	________	________	________	________	____
4.	________	________	________	________	________	____
5.	________	________	________	________	________	____

Results

Today's Profit Factor: ______

Today's PnL: ________________

Cumulative Profit Factor: ______

Cumulative PnL: ________________

Post-Trade

Did I follow my plan? What went right/wrong?

What were my emotions & mental during the trade?

What lessons did I learn?

What questions do I have after today's trades?

Was I correct in trading today or should I have just watched today?

Date: ________ Day: ________ Time: ______ Instrument: _____

Pre-Trade Checklist

☐ Reviewed News

☐ Reviewed Volume: ____________

☐ Reviewed VIX: ______

☐ Reviewed Open Interest: ____________

☐ Reviewed Fear/Greed Index: ____________

☐ Reviewed Direction: ____________

☐ My Target: ________

☐ My Risk/Reward: ________

☐ Am I trading during Prime Hours or a clear trend?: ________

Trade

Big Timeframe:	Medium Timeframe:	Small Timeframe:
____________	____________	____________
↑ ↔ ↓	↑ ↔ ↓	↑ ↔ ↓

	Contracts	Position	Entry Time	Entry Price	Exit Price	W/L
1.	________	________	________	________	________	____
2.	________	________	________	________	________	____
3.	________	________	________	________	________	____
4.	________	________	________	________	________	____
5.	________	________	________	________	________	____

Results

Today's Profit Factor: ______

Today's PnL: ________________

Cumulative Profit Factor: ______

Cumulative PnL: ________________

Post-Trade

Did I follow my plan? What went right/wrong?

What were my emotions & mental during the trade?

What lessons did I learn?

What questions do I have after today's trades?

Was I correct in trading today or should I have just watched today?

Date: ________ Day: ________ Time: ______ Instrument: _____

Pre-Trade Checklist

☐ Reviewed News

☐ Reviewed VIX: ______

☐ Reviewed Fear/Greed Index: ___________

☐ My Target: ________

☐ Reviewed Volume: ___________

☐ Reviewed Open Interest: ___________

☐ Reviewed Direction: ___________

☐ My Risk/Reward: ________

☐ Am I trading during Prime Hours or a clear trend?: _______

Trade

Big Timeframe:	Medium Timeframe:	Small Timeframe:
___________	___________	___________
↑ ↔ ↓	↑ ↔ ↓	↑ ↔ ↓

1. Contracts ______ Position ______ Entry Time ______ Entry Price ______ Exit Price ______ W/L ___
2. Contracts ______ Position ______ Entry Time ______ Entry Price ______ Exit Price ______ W/L ___
3. Contracts ______ Position ______ Entry Time ______ Entry Price ______ Exit Price ______ W/L ___
4. Contracts ______ Position ______ Entry Time ______ Entry Price ______ Exit Price ______ W/L ___
5. Contracts ______ Position ______ Entry Time ______ Entry Price ______ Exit Price ______ W/L ___

Results

Today's Profit Factor: ______ Today's PnL: _________________

Cumulative Profit Factor: ______ Cumulative PnL: _________________

Post-Trade

Did I follow my plan? What went right/wrong?

What were my emotions & mental during the trade?

What lessons did I learn?

What questions do I have after today's trades?

Was I correct in trading today or should I have just watched today?

Date: ________ Day: ________ Time: ______ Instrument: _____

Pre-Trade Checklist

☐ Reviewed News

☐ Reviewed Volume: ____________

☐ Reviewed VIX: ______

☐ Reviewed Open Interest: ____________

☐ Reviewed Fear/Greed Index: ___________

☐ Reviewed Direction: ____________

☐ My Target: ________

☐ My Risk/Reward: ________

☐ Am I trading during Prime Hours or a clear trend?: ________

Trade

Big Timeframe: ___________ ↑ ↔ ↓

Medium Timeframe: __________ ↑ ↔ ↓

Small Timeframe: ___________ ↑ ↔ ↓

	Contracts	Position	Entry Time	Entry Price	Exit Price	W/L
1.	________	_______	_________	_________	________	___
2.	________	_______	_________	_________	________	___
3.	________	_______	_________	_________	________	___
4.	________	_______	_________	_________	________	___
5.	________	_______	_________	_________	________	___

Results

Today's Profit Factor: ______ Today's PnL: _______________

Cumulative Profit Factor: ______ Cumulative PnL: _______________

Post-Trade

Did I follow my plan? What went right/wrong?

What were my emotions & mental during the trade?

What lessons did I learn?

What questions do I have after today's trades?

Was I correct in trading today or should I have just watched today?

Date: ________ Day: ________ Time: ______ Instrument: _____

Pre-Trade Checklist

☐ Reviewed News

☐ Reviewed VIX: ______

☐ Reviewed Fear/Greed Index: ___________

☐ My Target: ________

☐ Reviewed Volume: ___________

☐ Reviewed Open Interest: ___________

☐ Reviewed Direction: ___________

☐ My Risk/Reward: ________

☐ Am I trading during Prime Hours or a clear trend?: ________

Trade

Big Timeframe:	Medium Timeframe:	Small Timeframe:
___________	___________	___________
↑ ↔ ↓	↑ ↔ ↓	↑ ↔ ↓

1.	Contracts	Position	Entry Time	Entry Price	Exit Price	W/L
	________	_______	_________	_________	________	___
2.	Contracts	Position	Entry Time	Entry Price	Exit Price	W/L
	________	_______	_________	_________	________	___
3.	Contracts	Position	Entry Time	Entry Price	Exit Price	W/L
	________	_______	_________	_________	________	___
4.	Contracts	Position	Entry Time	Entry Price	Exit Price	W/L
	________	_______	_________	_________	________	___
5.	Contracts	Position	Entry Time	Entry Price	Exit Price	W/L
	________	_______	_________	_________	________	___

Results

Today's Profit Factor: ______ Today's PnL: ________________

Cumulative Profit Factor: ______ Cumulative PnL: ________________

Post-Trade

Did I follow my plan? What went right/wrong?

What were my emotions & mental during the trade?

What lessons did I learn?

What questions do I have after today's trades?

Was I correct in trading today or should I have just watched today?

Ten Habits with High ROI

1. Nutrition
2. Exercise
3. Mindfulness
4. Reading
5. Positive Mindset
6. Self-Control
7. Friendships
8. Family
9. Investing
10. Education

Date: ________ Day: ________ Time: ______ Instrument: _____

Pre-Trade Checklist

☐ Reviewed News

☐ Reviewed Volume: ____________

☐ Reviewed VIX: ______

☐ Reviewed Open Interest: ____________

☐ Reviewed Fear/Greed Index: ___________

☐ Reviewed Direction: ____________

☐ My Target: ________

☐ My Risk/Reward: ________

☐ Am I trading during Prime Hours or a clear trend?: ________

Trade

Big Timeframe:	Medium Timeframe:	Small Timeframe:
___________	__________	___________
↑ ↔ ↓	↑ ↔ ↓	↑ ↔ ↓

	Contracts	Position	Entry Time	Entry Price	Exit Price	W/L
1.	________	_______	_________	_________	________	___
2.	________	_______	_________	_________	________	___
3.	________	_______	_________	_________	________	___
4.	________	_______	_________	_________	________	___
5.	________	_______	_________	_________	________	___

Results

Today's Profit Factor: ______

Today's PnL: __________________

Cumulative Profit Factor: ______

Cumulative PnL: _________________

Post-Trade

Did I follow my plan? What went right/wrong?

What were my emotions & mental during the trade?

What lessons did I learn?

What questions do I have after today's trades?

Was I correct in trading today or should I have just watched today?

Date: ________ Day: ________ Time: ______ Instrument: _____

Pre-Trade Checklist

☐ Reviewed News

☐ Reviewed Volume: ____________

☐ Reviewed VIX: ______

☐ Reviewed Open Interest: ____________

☐ Reviewed Fear/Greed Index: ____________

☐ Reviewed Direction: ____________

☐ My Target: ________

☐ My Risk/Reward: ________

☐ Am I trading during Prime Hours or a clear trend?: ________

Trade

Big Timeframe:	Medium Timeframe:	Small Timeframe:
____________	____________	____________
↑ ↔ ↓	↑ ↔ ↓	↑ ↔ ↓

	Contracts	Position	Entry Time	Entry Price	Exit Price	W/L
1.	________	________	________	________	________	____
2.	________	________	________	________	________	____
3.	________	________	________	________	________	____
4.	________	________	________	________	________	____
5.	________	________	________	________	________	____

Results

Today's Profit Factor: ______ Today's PnL: ________________

Cumulative Profit Factor: ______ Cumulative PnL: ________________

Post-Trade

Did I follow my plan? What went right/wrong?

What were my emotions & mental during the trade?

What lessons did I learn?

What questions do I have after today's trades?

Was I correct in trading today or should I have just watched today?

Date: ________ Day: ________ Time: ______ Instrument: _____

Pre-Trade Checklist

☐ Reviewed News

☐ Reviewed VIX: ______

☐ Reviewed Fear/Greed Index: __________

☐ My Target: _______

☐ Reviewed Volume: __________

☐ Reviewed Open Interest: __________

☐ Reviewed Direction: __________

☐ My Risk/Reward: _______

☐ Am I trading during Prime Hours or a clear trend?: _______

Trade

Big Timeframe:	Medium Timeframe:	Small Timeframe:
__________	_________	__________
↑ ↔ ↓	↑ ↔ ↓	↑ ↔ ↓

1. Contracts ______ Position ______ Entry Time ______ Entry Price ______ Exit Price ______ W/L ___

2. Contracts ______ Position ______ Entry Time ______ Entry Price ______ Exit Price ______ W/L ___

3. Contracts ______ Position ______ Entry Time ______ Entry Price ______ Exit Price ______ W/L ___

4. Contracts ______ Position ______ Entry Time ______ Entry Price ______ Exit Price ______ W/L ___

5. Contracts ______ Position ______ Entry Time ______ Entry Price ______ Exit Price ______ W/L ___

Results

Today's Profit Factor: ______ Today's PnL: ________________

Cumulative Profit Factor: ______ Cumulative PnL: ________________

Post-Trade

Did I follow my plan? What went right/wrong?

What were my emotions & mental during the trade?

What lessons did I learn?

What questions do I have after today's trades?

Was I correct in trading today or should I have just watched today?

Date: ________ Day: ________ Time: ______ Instrument: _____

Pre-Trade Checklist

☐ Reviewed News

☐ Reviewed VIX: ______

☐ Reviewed Fear/Greed Index: ___________

☐ My Target: ________

☐ Reviewed Volume: ___________

☐ Reviewed Open Interest: ___________

☐ Reviewed Direction: ___________

☐ My Risk/Reward: ________

☐ Am I trading during Prime Hours or a clear trend?: ________

Trade

Big Timeframe:	Medium Timeframe:	Small Timeframe:
___________	___________	___________
↑ ↔ ↓	↑ ↔ ↓	↑ ↔ ↓

	Contracts	Position	Entry Time	Entry Price	Exit Price	W/L
1.	________	________	________	________	________	____
2.	________	________	________	________	________	____
3.	________	________	________	________	________	____
4.	________	________	________	________	________	____
5.	________	________	________	________	________	____

Results

Today's Profit Factor: ______ Today's PnL: _________________

Cumulative Profit Factor: ______ Cumulative PnL: _________________

Post-Trade

Did I follow my plan? What went right/wrong?

What were my emotions & mental during the trade?

What lessons did I learn?

What questions do I have after today's trades?

Was I correct in trading today or should I have just watched today?

Date: ________ Day: ________ Time: ______ Instrument: _____

Pre-Trade Checklist

☐ Reviewed News

☐ Reviewed VIX: ______

☐ Reviewed Fear/Greed Index: ___________

☐ My Target: ________

☐ Reviewed Volume: ___________

☐ Reviewed Open Interest: ___________

☐ Reviewed Direction: ___________

☐ My Risk/Reward: ________

☐ Am I trading during Prime Hours or a clear trend?: ________

Trade

Big Timeframe: ___________ ↑ ↔ ↓

Medium Timeframe: ___________ ↑ ↔ ↓

Small Timeframe: ___________ ↑ ↔ ↓

	Contracts	Position	Entry Time	Entry Price	Exit Price	W/L
1.	________	________	________	________	________	____
2.	________	________	________	________	________	____
3.	________	________	________	________	________	____
4.	________	________	________	________	________	____
5.	________	________	________	________	________	____

Results

Today's Profit Factor: ______ Today's PnL: _______________

Cumulative Profit Factor: ______ Cumulative PnL: _______________

Post-Trade

Did I follow my plan? What went right/wrong?

What were my emotions & mental during the trade?

What lessons did I learn?

What questions do I have after today's trades?

Was I correct in trading today or should I have just watched today?

EMA vs SMA

- 9 or 10 period: Very popular and extremely fast-moving. Often used as a directional filter

- 21 period: Medium-term/short-term swing trading and the most accurate moving average. Good when it comes to riding trends, price respects it so well, and it also signals trend shifts.

- 50 period: Long-term/standard swing-trading moving average, and best suited for identifying the longer-term direction. Most traders use it to ride trends because it's the ideal compromise between too short and too long term.

- 100 period: There is something about round numbers that attract traders, and that definitely holds true when it comes to the 100 moving average. It works very well for support and resistance – especially on the daily and/or weekly time frame

- 200 / 250 period: The same holds true for the 200 moving average. The 250 period moving average is popular on the daily chart since it describes one year of price action (one year has roughly 250 trading days)

Source: https://tradeciety.com/how-to-use-moving-averages/

Date: ________ Day: ________ Time: ______ Instrument: _____

Pre-Trade Checklist

☐ Reviewed News

☐ Reviewed VIX: ______

☐ Reviewed Fear/Greed Index: __________

☐ My Target: ________

☐ Reviewed Volume: __________

☐ Reviewed Open Interest: __________

☐ Reviewed Direction: __________

☐ My Risk/Reward: ________

☐ Am I trading during Prime Hours or a clear trend?: ________

Trade

Big Timeframe:	Medium Timeframe:	Small Timeframe:
__________	__________	__________
↑ ↔ ↓	↑ ↔ ↓	↑ ↔ ↓

1. Contracts ______ Position ______ Entry Time ______ Entry Price ______ Exit Price ______ W/L ___
2. Contracts ______ Position ______ Entry Time ______ Entry Price ______ Exit Price ______ W/L ___
3. Contracts ______ Position ______ Entry Time ______ Entry Price ______ Exit Price ______ W/L ___
4. Contracts ______ Position ______ Entry Time ______ Entry Price ______ Exit Price ______ W/L ___
5. Contracts ______ Position ______ Entry Time ______ Entry Price ______ Exit Price ______ W/L ___

Results

Today's Profit Factor: ______ Today's PnL: ______________

Cumulative Profit Factor: ______ Cumulative PnL: ______________

Post-Trade

Did I follow my plan? What went right/wrong?

What were my emotions & mental during the trade?

What lessons did I learn?

What questions do I have after today's trades?

Was I correct in trading today or should I have just watched today?

Date: ________ Day: ________ Time: ______ Instrument: _____

Pre-Trade Checklist

☐ Reviewed News

☐ Reviewed Volume: ____________

☐ Reviewed VIX: ______

☐ Reviewed Open Interest: ____________

☐ Reviewed Fear/Greed Index: ____________

☐ Reviewed Direction: ____________

☐ My Target: ________

☐ My Risk/Reward: ________

☐ Am I trading during Prime Hours or a clear trend?: ________

Trade

Big Timeframe:	Medium Timeframe:	Small Timeframe:
____________	____________	____________
↑ ↔ ↓	↑ ↔ ↓	↑ ↔ ↓

	Contracts	Position	Entry Time	Entry Price	Exit Price	W/L
1.	________	________	________	________	________	____
2.	________	________	________	________	________	____
3.	________	________	________	________	________	____
4.	________	________	________	________	________	____
5.	________	________	________	________	________	____

Results

Today's Profit Factor: ______ Today's PnL: ________________

Cumulative Profit Factor: ______ Cumulative PnL: ________________

Post-Trade

Did I follow my plan? What went right/wrong?

What were my emotions & mental during the trade?

What lessons did I learn?

What questions do I have after today's trades?

Was I correct in trading today or should I have just watched today?

Date: ________ Day: ________ Time: ______ Instrument: _____

Pre-Trade Checklist

☐ Reviewed News

☐ Reviewed VIX: ______

☐ Reviewed Fear/Greed Index: __________

☐ My Target: ________

☐ Reviewed Volume: __________

☐ Reviewed Open Interest: __________

☐ Reviewed Direction: __________

☐ My Risk/Reward: ________

☐ Am I trading during Prime Hours or a clear trend?: _______

Trade

Big Timeframe: __________ ↑ ↔ ↓

Medium Timeframe: __________ ↑ ↔ ↓

Small Timeframe: __________ ↑ ↔ ↓

	Contracts	Position	Entry Time	Entry Price	Exit Price	W/L
1.	______	______	______	______	______	___
2.	______	______	______	______	______	___
3.	______	______	______	______	______	___
4.	______	______	______	______	______	___
5.	______	______	______	______	______	___

Results

Today's Profit Factor: ______ Today's PnL: ______________

Cumulative Profit Factor: ______ Cumulative PnL: ______________

Post-Trade

Did I follow my plan? What went right/wrong?

What were my emotions & mental during the trade?

What lessons did I learn?

What questions do I have after today's trades?

Was I correct in trading today or should I have just watched today?

Date: ________ Day: ________ Time: ______ Instrument: ______

Pre-Trade Checklist

☐ Reviewed News

☐ Reviewed Volume: ____________

☐ Reviewed VIX: ______

☐ Reviewed Open Interest: ____________

☐ Reviewed Fear/Greed Index: ____________

☐ Reviewed Direction: ____________

☐ My Target: ________

☐ My Risk/Reward: ________

☐ Am I trading during Prime Hours or a clear trend?: ________

Trade

Big Timeframe: ____________ ↑ ↔ ↓

Medium Timeframe: ____________ ↑ ↔ ↓

Small Timeframe: ____________ ↑ ↔ ↓

	Contracts	Position	Entry Time	Entry Price	Exit Price	W/L
1.	______	______	______	______	______	___
2.	______	______	______	______	______	___
3.	______	______	______	______	______	___
4.	______	______	______	______	______	___
5.	______	______	______	______	______	___

Results

Today's Profit Factor: ______ Today's PnL: ____________

Cumulative Profit Factor: ______ Cumulative PnL: ____________

Post-Trade

Did I follow my plan? What went right/wrong?

What were my emotions & mental during the trade?

What lessons did I learn?

What questions do I have after today's trades?

Was I correct in trading today or should I have just watched today?

Date: ________ Day: ________ Time: ______ Instrument: ______

Pre-Trade Checklist

☐ Reviewed News

☐ Reviewed Volume: ____________

☐ Reviewed VIX: ______

☐ Reviewed Open Interest: ____________

☐ Reviewed Fear/Greed Index: ____________

☐ Reviewed Direction: ____________

☐ My Target: ________

☐ My Risk/Reward: ________

☐ Am I trading during Prime Hours or a clear trend?: ________

Trade

Big Timeframe:	Medium Timeframe:	Small Timeframe:
____________	____________	____________
↑ ↔ ↓	↑ ↔ ↓	↑ ↔ ↓

	Contracts	Position	Entry Time	Entry Price	Exit Price	W/L
1.	________	________	________	________	________	____
2.	________	________	________	________	________	____
3.	________	________	________	________	________	____
4.	________	________	________	________	________	____
5.	________	________	________	________	________	____

Results

Today's Profit Factor: ______ Today's PnL: ________________

Cumulative Profit Factor: ______ Cumulative PnL: ________________

Post-Trade

Did I follow my plan? What went right/wrong?

What were my emotions & mental during the trade?

What lessons did I learn?

What questions do I have after today's trades?

Was I correct in trading today or should I have just watched today?

Reading List

☐ PIT BULL: LESSONS FROM WALL STREET'S CHAMPION DAY TRADER by Martin Schwartz

☐ REMINISCENCES OF A STOCK OPERATOR by Edwin Lefèvre

☐ MARKET WIZARDS by Jack D. Schwager

☐ THE DISCIPLINED TRADER by Mark Douglas

☐ ONE GOOD TRADE by Mike Bellafiore

☐ THE COMPLETE TURTLE TRADER by Michael W. Covel

☐ TECHNICAL ANALYSIS OF THE FINANCIAL MARKETS by John J. Murphy

☐ TREND FOLLOWING by Michael W Covel

☐ GETTING STARTED IN TECHNICAL ANALYSIS by Jack D. Schwager

☐ TRADING IN THE ZONE by Mark Douglas

☐ THE LITTLE BOOK OF STOCK MARKET CYCLES by Jeffrey A. Hirsch

☐ READ AND PROFIT FROM FINANCIAL NEWS by Gerald Krefetz

Source: https://www.cmcmarkets.com/en/trading-guides/trading-strategies

Date: ________ Day: ________ Time: ______ Instrument: _____

Pre-Trade Checklist

☐ Reviewed News

☐ Reviewed VIX: ______

☐ Reviewed Fear/Greed Index: ___________

☐ My Target: ________

☐ Reviewed Volume: ___________

☐ Reviewed Open Interest: ___________

☐ Reviewed Direction: ___________

☐ My Risk/Reward: ________

☐ Am I trading during Prime Hours or a clear trend?: ________

Trade

Big Timeframe: ___________ ↑ ↔ ↓

Medium Timeframe: ___________ ↑ ↔ ↓

Small Timeframe: ___________ ↑ ↔ ↓

	Contracts	Position	Entry Time	Entry Price	Exit Price	W/L
1.	________	________	________	________	________	___
2.	________	________	________	________	________	___
3.	________	________	________	________	________	___
4.	________	________	________	________	________	___
5.	________	________	________	________	________	___

Results

Today's Profit Factor: ______ Today's PnL: ________________

Cumulative Profit Factor: ______ Cumulative PnL: ________________

Post-Trade

Did I follow my plan? What went right/wrong?

What were my emotions & mental during the trade?

What lessons did I learn?

What questions do I have after today's trades?

Was I correct in trading today or should I have just watched today?

Date: ________ Day: ________ Time: ______ Instrument: _____

Pre-Trade Checklist

☐ Reviewed News

☐ Reviewed Volume: ____________

☐ Reviewed VIX: ______

☐ Reviewed Open Interest: ____________

☐ Reviewed Fear/Greed Index: ___________

☐ Reviewed Direction: ____________

☐ My Target: ________

☐ My Risk/Reward: ________

☐ Am I trading during Prime Hours or a clear trend?: _______

Trade

Big Timeframe:	Medium Timeframe:	Small Timeframe:
___________	__________	___________
↑ ↔ ↓	↑ ↔ ↓	↑ ↔ ↓

	Contracts	Position	Entry Time	Entry Price	Exit Price	W/L
1.	________	_______	_________	_________	________	___
2.	________	_______	_________	_________	________	___
3.	________	_______	_________	_________	________	___
4.	________	_______	_________	_________	________	___
5.	________	_______	_________	_________	________	___

Results

Today's Profit Factor: ______

Today's PnL: ________________

Cumulative Profit Factor: ______

Cumulative PnL: ________________

Post-Trade

Did I follow my plan? What went right/wrong?

What were my emotions & mental during the trade?

What lessons did I learn?

What questions do I have after today's trades?

Was I correct in trading today or should I have just watched today?

Date: _________ Day: _________ Time: _______ Instrument: ______

Pre-Trade Checklist

☐ Reviewed News

☐ Reviewed Volume: ___________

☐ Reviewed VIX: ______

☐ Reviewed Open Interest: ___________

☐ Reviewed Fear/Greed Index: __________

☐ Reviewed Direction: ___________

☐ My Target: ________

☐ My Risk/Reward: ________

☐ Am I trading during Prime Hours or a clear trend?: ________

Trade

Big Timeframe:	Medium Timeframe:	Small Timeframe:
__________	__________	__________
↑ ↔ ↓	↑ ↔ ↓	↑ ↔ ↓

	Contracts	Position	Entry Time	Entry Price	Exit Price	W/L
1.	______	______	______	______	______	___
2.	______	______	______	______	______	___
3.	______	______	______	______	______	___
4.	______	______	______	______	______	___
5.	______	______	______	______	______	___

Results

Today's Profit Factor: ______ Today's PnL: _________________

Cumulative Profit Factor: ______ Cumulative PnL: ________________

Post-Trade

Did I follow my plan? What went right/wrong?

What were my emotions & mental during the trade?

What lessons did I learn?

What questions do I have after today's trades?

Was I correct in trading today or should I have just watched today?

Date: ________ Day: ________ Time: ______ Instrument: _____

Pre-Trade Checklist

☐ Reviewed News

☐ Reviewed VIX: ______

☐ Reviewed Fear/Greed Index: ___________

☐ My Target: ________

☐ Reviewed Volume: ___________

☐ Reviewed Open Interest: ___________

☐ Reviewed Direction: ___________

☐ My Risk/Reward: ________

☐ Am I trading during Prime Hours or a clear trend?: ________

Trade

Big Timeframe: ___________ ↑ ↔ ↓

Medium Timeframe: ___________ ↑ ↔ ↓

Small Timeframe: ___________ ↑ ↔ ↓

	Contracts	Position	Entry Time	Entry Price	Exit Price	W/L
1.	________	_______	_________	_________	________	___
2.	________	_______	_________	_________	________	___
3.	________	_______	_________	_________	________	___
4.	________	_______	_________	_________	________	___
5.	________	_______	_________	_________	________	___

Results

Today's Profit Factor: ______ Today's PnL: _________________

Cumulative Profit Factor: ______ Cumulative PnL: ________________

Post-Trade

Did I follow my plan? What went right/wrong?

What were my emotions & mental during the trade?

What lessons did I learn?

What questions do I have after today's trades?

Was I correct in trading today or should I have just watched today?

Date: ________ Day: ________ Time: ______ Instrument: ______

Pre-Trade Checklist

☐ Reviewed News

☐ Reviewed Volume: ____________

☐ Reviewed VIX: ______

☐ Reviewed Open Interest: ____________

☐ Reviewed Fear/Greed Index: ____________

☐ Reviewed Direction: ____________

☐ My Target: ________

☐ My Risk/Reward: ________

☐ Am I trading during Prime Hours or a clear trend?: ________

Trade

Big Timeframe:	Medium Timeframe:	Small Timeframe:
____________	____________	____________
↑ ↔ ↓	↑ ↔ ↓	↑ ↔ ↓

	Contracts	Position	Entry Time	Entry Price	Exit Price	W/L
1.	________	________	________	________	________	____
2.	________	________	________	________	________	____
3.	________	________	________	________	________	____
4.	________	________	________	________	________	____
5.	________	________	________	________	________	____

Results

Today's Profit Factor: ______ Today's PnL: ________________

Cumulative Profit Factor: ______ Cumulative PnL: ________________

Post-Trade

Did I follow my plan? What went right/wrong?

What were my emotions & mental during the trade?

What lessons did I learn?

What questions do I have after today's trades?

Was I correct in trading today or should I have just watched today?

Homework:
Day Trading
8, 13, 21 EMA Strategy

Three different periods (8,13, 21) EMA will help you to identify trends at the beginning when it starts to form. It works fine at any time frame chart of the financial assets. You can create a complete trading strategy by using these EMA signal lines. For more accuracy, you can combine these EMA signal lines with other technical indicators such as parabolic SAR, Volume, MACD, RSI, etc.

Bullish trade setup

Bearish trade setup

Source: https://fxtechlab.com/8-13-21-ema-strategy/

Date: ________ Day: ________ Time: ______ Instrument: _____

Pre-Trade Checklist

☐ Reviewed News

☐ Reviewed VIX: ______

☐ Reviewed Fear/Greed Index: ___________

☐ My Target: ________

☐ Reviewed Volume: ___________

☐ Reviewed Open Interest: ___________

☐ Reviewed Direction: ___________

☐ My Risk/Reward: ________

☐ Am I trading during Prime Hours or a clear trend?: _______

Trade

Big Timeframe:	Medium Timeframe:	Small Timeframe:
___________	___________	___________
↑ ↔ ↓	↑ ↔ ↓	↑ ↔ ↓

	Contracts	Position	Entry Time	Entry Price	Exit Price	W/L
1.	________	_______	_________	_________	________	___
2.	________	_______	_________	_________	________	___
3.	________	_______	_________	_________	________	___
4.	________	_______	_________	_________	________	___
5.	________	_______	_________	_________	________	___

Results

Today's Profit Factor: ______ Today's PnL: _________________

Cumulative Profit Factor: ______ Cumulative PnL: ________________

Post-Trade

Did I follow my plan? What went right/wrong?

What were my emotions & mental during the trade?

What lessons did I learn?

What questions do I have after today's trades?

Was I correct in trading today or should I have just watched today?

Date: ________ Day: ________ Time: ______ Instrument: _____

Pre-Trade Checklist

☐ Reviewed News

☐ Reviewed Volume: ____________

☐ Reviewed VIX: ______

☐ Reviewed Open Interest: ____________

☐ Reviewed Fear/Greed Index: ____________

☐ Reviewed Direction: ____________

☐ My Target: ________

☐ My Risk/Reward: ________

☐ Am I trading during Prime Hours or a clear trend?: ________

Trade

Big Timeframe:	Medium Timeframe:	Small Timeframe:
____________	____________	____________
↑ ↔ ↓	↑ ↔ ↓	↑ ↔ ↓

	Contracts	Position	Entry Time	Entry Price	Exit Price	W/L
1.	________	________	________	________	________	____
2.	________	________	________	________	________	____
3.	________	________	________	________	________	____
4.	________	________	________	________	________	____
5.	________	________	________	________	________	____

Results

Today's Profit Factor: ______

Today's PnL: ________________

Cumulative Profit Factor: ______

Cumulative PnL: ________________

Post-Trade

Did I follow my plan? What went right/wrong?

What were my emotions & mental during the trade?

What lessons did I learn?

What questions do I have after today's trades?

Was I correct in trading today or should I have just watched today?

Date: ________ Day: ________ Time: ______ Instrument: ______

Pre-Trade Checklist

☐ Reviewed News

☐ Reviewed VIX: ______

☐ Reviewed Fear/Greed Index: ___________

☐ My Target: ________

☐ Reviewed Volume: ___________

☐ Reviewed Open Interest: ___________

☐ Reviewed Direction: ___________

☐ My Risk/Reward: ________

☐ Am I trading during Prime Hours or a clear trend?: ________

Trade

Big Timeframe: ___________	Medium Timeframe: __________	Small Timeframe: ___________
↑ ↔ ↓	↑ ↔ ↓	↑ ↔ ↓

	Contracts	Position	Entry Time	Entry Price	Exit Price	W/L
1.	________	________	________	________	________	____
2.	________	________	________	________	________	____
3.	________	________	________	________	________	____
4.	________	________	________	________	________	____
5.	________	________	________	________	________	____

Results

Today's Profit Factor: ______ Today's PnL: _______________

Cumulative Profit Factor: ______ Cumulative PnL: _______________

Post-Trade

Did I follow my plan? What went right/wrong?

What were my emotions & mental during the trade?

What lessons did I learn?

What questions do I have after today's trades?

Was I correct in trading today or should I have just watched today?

Date: ________ Day: ________ Time: ______ Instrument: _____

Pre-Trade Checklist

☐ Reviewed News

☐ Reviewed Volume: ____________

☐ Reviewed VIX: ______

☐ Reviewed Open Interest: ____________

☐ Reviewed Fear/Greed Index: ____________

☐ Reviewed Direction: ____________

☐ My Target: ________

☐ My Risk/Reward: ________

☐ Am I trading during Prime Hours or a clear trend?: ________

Trade

Big Timeframe:	Medium Timeframe:	Small Timeframe:
____________	___________	____________
↑ ↔ ↓	↑ ↔ ↓	↑ ↔ ↓

1. Contracts ________ Position ________ Entry Time __________ Entry Price __________ Exit Price _________ W/L ____
2. Contracts ________ Position ________ Entry Time __________ Entry Price __________ Exit Price _________ W/L ____
3. Contracts ________ Position ________ Entry Time __________ Entry Price __________ Exit Price _________ W/L ____
4. Contracts ________ Position ________ Entry Time __________ Entry Price __________ Exit Price _________ W/L ____
5. Contracts ________ Position ________ Entry Time __________ Entry Price __________ Exit Price _________ W/L ____

Results

Today's Profit Factor: ______ Today's PnL: ________________

Cumulative Profit Factor: ______ Cumulative PnL: ________________

Post-Trade

Did I follow my plan? What went right/wrong?

What were my emotions & mental during the trade?

What lessons did I learn?

What questions do I have after today's trades?

Was I correct in trading today or should I have just watched today?

Date: ________ Day: ________ Time: ______ Instrument: _____

Pre-Trade Checklist

☐ Reviewed News

☐ Reviewed Volume: ____________

☐ Reviewed VIX: ______

☐ Reviewed Open Interest: ____________

☐ Reviewed Fear/Greed Index: __________

☐ Reviewed Direction: ____________

☐ My Target: ________

☐ My Risk/Reward: ________

☐ Am I trading during Prime Hours or a clear trend?: ________

Trade

Big Timeframe:	Medium Timeframe:	Small Timeframe:
__________	__________	__________
↑ ↔ ↓	↑ ↔ ↓	↑ ↔ ↓

	Contracts	Position	Entry Time	Entry Price	Exit Price	W/L
1.	________	________	________	________	________	____
2.	________	________	________	________	________	____
3.	________	________	________	________	________	____
4.	________	________	________	________	________	____
5.	________	________	________	________	________	____

Results

Today's Profit Factor: ______ Today's PnL: ________________

Cumulative Profit Factor: ______ Cumulative PnL: ________________

Post-Trade

Did I follow my plan? What went right/wrong?

What were my emotions & mental during the trade?

What lessons did I learn?

What questions do I have after today's trades?

Was I correct in trading today or should I have just watched today?

Notes

Notes

Notes

Notes

Notes

Notes

Notes

Notes

Notes

Notes

Notes

Notes

Made in United States
North Haven, CT
04 November 2026

21730642R10055